Unraveling Human Nature

A Comprehensive Guide to Theories of Personality Development

Freudian Trips

Copyright Page

Disclaimer

The views and opinions expressed in this book are those of the author(s) and do not necessarily reflect the official policy or position of any other agency, organization, employer, or company. The contents of this book are for informational and educational purposes only and are not intended to serve as professional advice, diagnosis, or treatment.

The information provided in this book is believed to be accurate and reliable as of the date of publication. However, it may include some errors or inaccuracies, and no warranty or guarantee is provided regarding the accuracy, timeliness, or applicability of the content.

Readers are encouraged to consult with professional philosophers, educators, or other qualified professionals where appropriate for personalized advice. The author(s) and publisher shall not be liable for any loss, damage, or harm caused or alleged to be caused, directly or indirectly, by the information or ideas contained, suggested, or referenced in this book.

By reading this book, the reader acknowledges and agrees that they are solely responsible for how they interpret and apply the information contained herein.

This book may also include references to other works, studies, and sources. These references are provided for further reading and exploration and do not imply endorsement or validation of the specific theories, viewpoints, or interpretations presented in those works.

Chapter 1: An Introduction to the Wonders of Personality

Defining Personality: More Than Just a Label

Have you ever been called "outgoing" or "shy"? Perhaps someone has remarked that you have a "sunny" disposition or that you're incredibly "meticulous." These are all traits, tiny facets of the dazzling diamond that is your personality. But what exactly is personality?

In essence, personality refers to the distinctive collection of traits, proclivities, attitudes, and patterns that constitute an individual. It's the essence of who you are, the consistent patterns in how you behave, think, and feel. It's why you might be inclined to strike up a conversation with a stranger, or why you might prefer to sit back and observe. Think of it as your personal fingerprint in the world of behavior and interaction.

A Brief Walk Through Time: The Study of Personality

The fascination with personality isn't a new trend of the 21st century. Humans have been intrigued by individual differences for centuries! From ancient philosophers musing about human nature to modern psychologists developing intricate theories, the quest to understand 'why we are the way we are' has always been in vogue.

Historically, many cultures believed that personality was influenced by the balance of bodily fluids or the position of stars at birth. Fast forward to the Renaissance, and we encounter the idea that physical appearance, like the shape of one's head, could determine character traits.

The study of personality did not start to take on a scientific shape until the late 19th and early 20th centuries. Pioneers like Sigmund Freud explored the depths of the human psyche, while others, like B.F. Skinner, looked at how our environments shape us. The journey to understand personality has been, and continues to be, a vibrant tapestry of insights, theories, and stories.

Why It Matters: The Role of Personality in Our Lives

Now, you might be thinking, "That's all well and good, but why should I care about personality theories?" The answer is simple: understanding personality development can greatly enrich our lives.

Self-awareness: By understanding the facets of our personality, we can better comprehend our strengths, weaknesses, desires, and fears. It's like being handed a manual to ourselves. Imagine navigating life with a clearer understanding of why certain situations energize you while others drain you.

Relationships: Ever had a clash with someone and wondered, "Why can't they see things my way?" Understanding personality can bridge the gap in interpersonal conflicts, leading to deeper, more fulfilling relationships.

Career Choices: Some of us thrive in dynamic, ever-changing environments, while others prefer methodical, structured tasks. Recognizing our personality traits can guide us towards careers where we'll naturally excel.

Personal Growth: With awareness comes the potential for growth. Recognizing certain patterns in our behavior, we can make informed decisions about changes we might want to make.

In the chapters that follow, we'll embark on a journey through various theories of personality. From the dreamy depths of the psychoanalytic approach to the grounded realities of the behaviorists, we'll explore the many lenses through which humanity has tried to understand its nature. So, buckle up! It's going to be an enlightening ride.

Chapter 2: Peeking Behind the Curtain: The World of Psychoanalysis

Enter Sigmund Freud: The Father of Psychoanalysis

Picture this: Vienna, late 19th century. The world was buzzing with new ideas, and in this vibrant setting, a curious doctor named Sigmund Freud began to question the mysteries of the human mind. His ideas, considered radical at the time, laid the foundation for what we now know as psychoanalytic theories.

The Three Musketeers of Personality: Id, Ego, and Superego

Freud believed that our personality is like an iceberg, with the majority hidden beneath the surface. Dive a little deeper, and you'll find three major players:

Id: Think of this as a toddler inside us, demanding immediate satisfaction. It's driven by desires and urges without any concern for reality or morality. If you've ever felt an impulse to eat that last slice of cake, you've felt the Id in action.

Ego: The mediator. It tries to balance the demands of the Id with the realities of the world. Like a responsible older sibling, the Ego knows we can't always get what we want immediately and looks for realistic ways to satisfy our desires.

Superego: The moral compass. It's like a strict teacher or parent, always urging us to behave properly and chastising us when we don't. It represents our sense of right and wrong.

Together, these three forces interact and influence our thoughts, feelings, and actions.

Journey Through Childhood: Freud's Psychosexual Stages

Freud believed that our personality develops in stages, each centered around a specific part of the body that provides pleasure:

Oral Stage (Birth to 1 year): Pleasure centers on the mouth. Ever noticed how babies love to put everything in their mouths?

Anal Stage (1 to 3 years): Here, toddlers derive pleasure from holding in or letting go of their bodily wastes. This is also when potty training happens.

Phallic Stage (3 to 6 years): Children become curious about their bodies and the differences between boys and girls.

Latency Stage (6 years to puberty): Sexual impulses lie dormant, and children focus on hobbies, school, and same-sex friendships.

Genital Stage (Puberty onward): This is when people start to form romantic relationships with others.

Freud believed that challenges or over-indulgence in any of these stages could lead to personality issues in adulthood.

Guarding the Fortress: Defense Mechanisms

Ever forgotten an unpleasant memory or justified a bad decision? According to Freud, these are defense mechanisms—ways our Ego protects itself from distressing thoughts or feelings. They're like the walls and moats around a castle, shielding it from threats.

Freud's Legacy: Praises and Puzzles

No doubt, Freud's ideas were groundbreaking. He introduced the idea that our childhood experiences deeply influence our adult lives. He gave us tools to explore our unconscious mind and understand our dreams.

However, not everyone agreed with everything he said. Critics pointed out that his theories were based on a small, specific group of patients. Some thought he focused too much on sexuality. Others believed that his theories couldn't be scientifically tested.

Beyond Freud: The Neo-Freudians

While Freud was a trailblazer, many of his students and followers began to branch out, forming their own ideas. These thinkers, often called "Neo-Freudians," agreed with some of Freud's ideas but introduced their own twists:

Carl Jung believed in a collective unconscious, shared by all humans, filled with myths and symbols.

Alfred Adler focused on the importance of feelings of inferiority and the drive to overcome them.

Karen Horney criticized Freud's views on women and highlighted the role of social relationships in shaping personality.

As we wrap up this chapter, remember: while the world of psychoanalysis might seem complex, it's all about understanding the unseen forces that shape our thoughts, feelings, and behaviors. Whether you're Team Freud or a Neo-Freudian fan, there's no denying the profound impact these ideas have had on our understanding of the human psyche.

Chapter 3: Behaviorism: Personality Shaped by External Forces

If psychoanalysts were obsessed with our inner world, the behaviorists kept their eyes glued on external forces. For them, personality was less like a bubbling cauldron and more like a sculptor chipping away at stone. Our environments shape us through reinforcement, punishment, and observation.

B.F. Skinner and Operant Conditioning

Burrhus Frederic (call me B.F.) Skinner saw personalities forming through "operant conditioning." Like playing a giant pinball machine, our behaviors bump into rewards and punishments, which determine their likelihood of repeating. Reinforcement (both positive and negative) increases a behavior's frequency. For example, a child cries until given candy, learning that tantrums merit treats. Punishment decreases behaviors by introducing unpleasant consequences. Say a teenager stays out late and gets grounded, making it less likely they'll break curfew again.

Skinner viewed personalities as collections of reinforced and punished behavioral patterns. Environments coax out certain traits through reinforcement schedules. Surround someone with frequent praise, and watch agreeableness bloom. Punish every mistake, and neuroticism may take root. For Skinner, personality was largely a product of external conditioning.

John B. Watson and Classical Conditioning

John B. Watson also saw personality development as environmentally determined. But instead of reinforcement, he focused on classical conditioning - learning associations between stimuli and reflexive responses. His famous "Little Albert" experiment (which would raise ethical concerns today) showed how fear could be classically conditioned. Watson viewed personalities as conditioned emotional responses.

Watson also emphasized social learning theory - we observe "role models" and imitate their behavior. Watching your confident friend speak up in groups reinforces being outgoing. Observing your cautious sibling leads to observational learning of inhibition. According to Watson, we partially construct our personalities by copying others.

While intuitively compelling, strict behaviorism faced criticism. Could human complexity really be reduced to simple stimulus-response links? Nonetheless, behaviorism helped demonstrate how external forces shape our inner lives in subtle yet profound ways.

Chapter 4: The Humanistic Journey: Understanding Our Best Selves

A Fresh Perspective: Enter Humanistic Theories

Imagine a world where the focus is not on our problems or our past, but on our potential and the best version of ourselves. Welcome to the realm of humanistic theories! Rather than digging deep into our unconscious or looking at our behavior in response to our environment, humanistic theories celebrate our conscious experiences, free will, and the quest for personal growth.

Carl Rogers: Seeing the Person in Front of You

In a world filled with experts and authority figures, Carl Rogers stood out. He believed that each of us is the best expert on our own lives. Let's unravel his main ideas:

The Self-Concept: Picture a mental mirror. When you look into it, you see your reflection, not just physically but in terms of beliefs, feelings, and thoughts about yourself. This is your self-concept. It's how you see yourself, and it plays a major role in how you feel and act. When our self-concept aligns with our experiences, we feel harmonious. But if there's a mismatch, we can feel anxious.

Self-Actualization: Imagine a seed. Given the right conditions - water, sunlight, and good soil - it grows into a robust plant. Humans, Rogers believed, are quite similar. We all have an innate drive to grow, to reach our fullest potential, to "blossom." This journey towards our best selves is what Rogers called self-actualization.

Unconditional Positive Regard: Think back to a time when someone listened to you without judgment, offering pure under-standing and acceptance, no strings attached. That's unconditional positive regard. Rogers believed that to truly flourish, we need envi-ronments that provide this kind of acceptance, where we are loved for who we are, not for what we do.

Abraham Maslow: Climbing the Ladder of Needs

If Rogers introduced us to the idea of becoming our best selves, Abraham Maslow gave us a roadmap. His famous Hierarchy of Needs is often pictured as a pyramid, and here's a simple breakdown:

Basic Human Needs: At the base of the pyramid, we have our physiological needs: food, water, sleep, and warmth. Just above these are our needs for safety and security.

Belonging and Love: Once our basic needs are met, we yearn for social connections, friendships, and romantic relationships.

Esteem: This is about feeling respected, recognized for our achievements, and having a sense of self-worth.

Self-Actualization: At the very top of the pyramid, this is our quest to achieve our personal potential and creativity. It's about becoming the best version of ourselves.

Maslow believed that to reach the top, we need to ensure the lower levels of the pyramid are well-supported. It's tough to think about self-fulfillment if you're constantly hungry or feeling unsafe.

Reflecting on Humanistic Theories

Humanistic theories brought a breath of fresh air to the world of psychology. They emphasized optimism, potential, and the importance of the individual experience.

However, like all theories, they have their critics. Some argue that these theories are too idealistic or that they don't consider the darker sides of human nature. Others feel they're too Western-centric and might not apply universally.

But despite these critiques, the core message of humanistic theories remains powerful: that each of us has a unique potential, and given the right environment and understanding, we can flourish and shine.

As you move forward, remember the essence of humanistic theories: We're all on a journey to become our best selves, and with understanding, acceptance, and a focus on our potential, we can make that journey meaningful.

Chapter 5: Cognitive Theories: Mind Over Matter

While behaviorists focused on external conditioning, cognitive theorists opened the black box of the mind. They argued that personality isn't just shaped by outward reinforcement - our inner thoughts and beliefs also sculpt who we become.

Albert Bandura's Social Cognitive Theory

Canadian psychologist Albert Bandura integrated behavioral and cognitive insights. Like Watson, he believed in observational learning - we learn by aping role models. But Bandura argued that first we mentally represent others' behavior symbolically. Personality, therefore, depends on how we actively process and imitate our social environment.

Bandura also introduced the influential idea of self-efficacy - our level of confidence to exercise control and master challenges. Those with high self-efficacy see themselves accomplishing goals. They develop traits like proactivity and perseverance. Those with low self-efficacy avoid challenges, undermining their potential. According to Bandura, belief in our abilities plays a key role in personality development.

Cognitive-Behavioral Approaches

Cognitive behavioral theorists further explored the link between thought patterns and personality. They found that certain thinking styles, like all-or-nothing thinking, fuel personality traits like neuroticism. Through cognitive restructuring - intentionally shifting thought patterns - we can positively change our personality. In behaviorism, the environment shapes you. Here, you shape yourself by reshaping your mental environment.

While cognitive theories illuminated the active mind's role in personality, they faced criticism for underestimating inborn temperaments. However, they remain highly influential, especially in therapy.

Chapter 6: The Building Blocks of You: Exploring Trait Theories

Setting the Stage: What Are Traits?

Imagine your personality as a vast canvas, painted with a myriad of colors. Each color represents a different characteristic, quality, or behavior. These "colors" are what we refer to as traits. They are consistent patterns in our behavior, thoughts, and emotions that make us uniquely us.

Gordon Allport: The Pioneering Palette of Traits

In the bustling world of personality theories, Gordon Allport emerged with a fresh perspective. He believed that to understand humans, we should focus on the present, not the past, and on the individual, not the group.

Cardinal Traits: These are dominant traits that define a person's life. Think of Mother Teresa and her compassion or Martin Luther King Jr. and his quest for justice. Not everyone has a cardinal trait, but when they do, it's hard to miss.

Central Traits: These are the broad traits that serve as the framework for our personalities. qualities such as sincerity, anxiety, or extroversion. It is comparable to the fundamental hues of our canvas.

Secondary Traits: These are more situational. They might only appear in certain circumstances. For instance, you might be incredibly patient in your professional life but not while waiting in a long queue for coffee.

Allport viewed these traits as the building blocks of our personality, uniquely combined in each individual.

Raymond Cattell: A More Detailed Sketch

While Allport gave us a broad brush, Raymond Cattell came along with a fine-tipped pen. He wanted to dive deeper, to offer a more detailed description of personality.

Identifying and Measuring Personality Traits: Cattell believed that our personalities are composed of a set of specific traits. Using a method called factor analysis, he distilled human personality into 16 key traits, ranging from warmth and emotional stability to sensitivity and vigilance.

Traits and Behavior Prediction: Cattell's goal wasn't just to list these traits but to understand how they interact to predict our behavior. For instance, someone scoring high on "warmth" and "social boldness" might be predicted to be a lively and engaging party guest.

Modern Musings: Contemporary Trait Theories

The world of trait theories didn't stop with Allport and Cattell. Researchers continued to explore, refine, and expand:

The Big Five: Today, one of the most popular trait models is the Big Five, which distills personality into five core traits: Openness, Conscientiousness, Extraversion, Agreeableness, and Neuroticism. It's like a modern, streamlined version of Cattell's model.

Situational Factors: Modern researchers also recognize that while traits are consistent, they can be influenced by our environment. Just like how a color might appear different under various lighting conditions, our traits might manifest differently in different situations.

As we wrap up this chapter, remember that trait theories offer a fascinating lens to view our personalities. They suggest that we're all composed of a unique mix of traits, a distinctive palette of colors that makes us who we are. As you go about your day, think about the traits that shine through in different situations. It's a journey of self-discovery, one brushstroke at a time.

Chapter 7: Biological Theories: It's In Our Nature

In contrast to learning theories, biological models propose that personality is wired into our nature. While environments shape us, our genes and brains come pre-packaged with personality tendencies. Evidence suggests nature and nurture collaborate in shaping who we become.

Genetic Influences

Studies of identical twins reared apart reveal striking personality commonalities, suggesting genetic origins. Heritability estimates attribute 40-60% of personality variation to genetic factors. Specific gene variants have been weakly linked to traits like novelty-seeking and aggression.

However, there are no "genes for" complex traits like neuroticism. Rather, hundreds or thousands of genes likely contribute to personality dispositions, which then interact with environments. So while personalities run in families, genetic forces alone cannot determine who we become.

Brain Structures

Biological theorists have also proposed brain mechanisms underlying personality. The neurotransmitter serotonin has been linked to traits like agreeableness. Differences in regional brain volumes correlate with qualities like openness and conscientiousness. fMRI scans show distinctive patterns of brain activation in people with different temperaments.

However, the causal direction is unclear - do brain differences shape personality, or does personality impact the brain? Most evidence suggests bidirectional influence.

The Nature vs Nurture Debate

The complex interplay of genetic and environmental forces in personality remains a lively scientific debate. But rather than an "either/or", today most experts agree it's "both/and". Personality arises from an intricate dance between the nature we're born with, and the nurture we encounter.

Chapter 8: Weaving Together the Threads: Integrative Approaches to Personality

A Tapestry of Understanding: The Integrative Approach

Imagine a grand quilt, each patch representing a different theory of personality. Individually, each patch is beautiful and informative. But when woven together, they create a richer, fuller understanding of human nature. This is the essence of integrative approaches. Instead of sticking to just one theory, integrative approaches blend the best parts of many to create a holistic view of personality.

The Multi-Faceted Crystal: Multi-Factor Models of Personality

Our personalities are intricate, shaped by countless factors and experiences. Recognizing this complexity, researchers have developed multi-factor models.

Combining Different Theoretical Perspectives: Just as a chef might combine ingredients from various cuisines to create a fusion dish, multi-factor models integrate concepts from different theories. This could mean blending the structured stages of psychoanalytic theories with the free-willed optimism of humanistic theories, or the environmental focus of behavioral theories with the inherited aspects of biological theories.

Understanding the Complexity of Personality: By looking at personality through multiple lenses, we get a more nuanced understanding. It's like viewing a gemstone from various angles, each perspective revealing a new facet.

Bringing Theories to Life: Implications for Personal Growth and Well-Being

Understanding personality isn't just an academic exercise. It has real, tangible benefits for our personal and collective well-being.

Applying Personality Theories in Real Life: By understanding what makes us "tick", we can make more informed decisions, from career choices to hobbies. For instance, if we recognize our need for social connections (a la Maslow), we might prioritize team sports or group activities.

Enhancing Self-Understanding and Relationships: Ever had a 'light bulb' moment when you suddenly understand why you behave a certain way? Or why someone you know acts the way they do? Integrating different personality theories can provide these insights, paving the way for better self-awareness and more harmonious relationships.

Gazing into the Future: The Next Steps in Personality Research

The journey of understanding personality is ongoing. As we advance in technology, methodology, and societal understanding, the realm of personality research continues to expand and evolve.

Neuroscience and Personality: With tools like brain imaging, we're beginning to see how personality traits might be reflected in our brain's structure and function.

Cultural and Global Perspectives: As our world becomes more interconnected, there's a growing interest in understanding personality across different cultures. Are the Big Five traits universal? How do societal values shape personality?

Digital Footprints: In our digital age, researchers are exploring how our online behaviors, from social media posts to browser histories, might offer insights into our personalities.

In conclusion, the integrative approach to personality is like assembling a jigsaw puzzle. Each piece, representing a different theory or perspective, is essential. And as we fit them together, we get a beautiful, intricate picture of human nature. As you continue your journey of self-discovery, remember that you are a blend of many factors, experiences, and traits. Celebrate the complexity, for it is what makes you, uniquely you.

Chapter 9: Personality In All Its Glory

In our journey through the halls of personality theories, we've encountered many perspectives on our diverse human nature. Psychoanalysts revealed inner conflicts, while humanists embraced our highest potentials. Behaviorists showed how surroundings shape us, as cognitive theorists illuminated our thinking patterns. Biologists demonstrated nature's role in temperament.

Each lens provides insights into the multifaceted diamond that is personality. Psychoanalytic notions of defense mechanisms explain avoidant tendencies. Learning theories account for how reinforcement molds our sociability. Cognitive approaches help anxious rumination. Biological models describe inborn introversion.

But while theories divide personality into discrete slices, our actual personalities blend these elements like a swirling stew. Nature and nurture interactively guide our trajectory. Environment and biology, thought and emotion, all dance together to form the unique constellation of each person.

So personality isn't static - it dynamically evolves throughout our lives. We shape our traits, and they shape us, in a reciprocal exchange. With deeper understanding, we can better navigate ourselves, appreciating both our ingrained dispositions and flexibility to grow.

Our personality journey reveals above all the complexity of being human. Through integrated insights, may we fulfill the ancient dictum: "Know thyself." For self-knowledge breeds both compassion for oneself and others.

About Freudian Trips

Welcome to Freudian Trips, your dedicated platform for diving deep into the world of psychology. We are more than just a YouTube channel or a book publisher. We are a beacon of enlightenment, making complex psychological concepts accessible and engaging for all.

Our YouTube channel is a rich repository of psychology made simple. We take the profound and often complex ideas from the world of psychology and break them down into digestible, easy-to-understand content. From the foundational theories of Freud to the cognitive insights of Piaget, we cover a broad spectrum of psychological schools and thoughts, making psychology accessible to everyone, regardless of their background or prior knowledge.

As a book publisher, we take the same approach, transforming intricate psychological theories into comprehensible narratives. Our books are not just collections of words, but vessels of wisdom that make psychology approachable and relatable. We believe that psychology should not be confined to academic circles, but should be available to all who seek to understand the human mind and behavior.

At Freudian Trips, we believe in the power of curiosity and the pursuit of knowledge. We are here to stoke the fires of your curiosity, to guide you on your intellectual journey, and to help you navigate the fascinating world of psychology.

If you are someone who is not afraid to question, to explore, and to learn, then you are in the right place. Join us on this journey of exploration, as we make psychology easy to understand, one concept at a time.

Be sure to visit our Youtube channel at: www.freudiantrips.com/youtube

You can also visit us on the web at www.freudiantrips.com

Welcome to The Freudian Trip community. Stay curious. Stay enlightened.